3D PRINTING GUIDE

FOR **NEWCOMERS**

Simple steps for learning how to use a 3D printer, including tips and tricks for maintaining and troubleshooting your 3D printer

Stephen W. Rock

Copyright © 2019

Dedicated to all my readers

Acknowledgement

Ii want to say a very big thank you to Michael Lime, a 3D builder, my colleague. He gave me moral support throughout the process of writing this book.

Table of Contents

INTRODUCTION 8
CHAPTER 1 9
INTRODUCTION TO 3D PRINTING 9
What really is 3D Printing? 12
How a 3D printer works 12
Applications of 3D Printing 14
Home uses of a 3D printer 16
Design for 3D Printing 17
CHAPTER 2 19
GETTING STARTED WITH 3D PRINTING 19
Do you need a 3D printer really? 19
What if you decide to make your own models? 20
Is it possible to scan real objects and print them? 21
How can you print downloaded models? 21
How do you print models that you created? 22
CHAPTER 3 24
HOW TO PRINT IN MULT-COLOR WITH A SINGLE EXTRUDER 24
CHAPTER 4 29

3D PRINTING TIPS 29

CHAPTER 5 33

COMMON 3D PRINTING TROUBLESHOOTING PROBLEMS AND SOLUTIONS 33

Troubleshooting for MatterControl Print Leveling 33

CHAPTER 6 38

TOOLS THAT WILL HELP YOU BECOME A 3D ORINTING PRO 38

CHAPTER 7 42

3D PRINTING RESOURCES 42

3D Model Sites 42

Free 3D Design Software 43

CHAPTER 8 44

MAINTAINING YOUR 3D PRINTER 44

What you must never do with your 3D printer 47

CHAPTER 9 49

BEGINNERS LESSONS TO FOR USING SKETCHUP 49

CHAPTER 10 53

HOW TO HANDLE BASIC 2D DRAWINGS – LINES, CIRCLES, RECTANGLES 53

CONCLUSION 56

DISCLAIMER 58

ABOUT THE AUTHOR 59

INTRODUCTION

In a time like this where 3D design and printing is a skill that many people wish to acquire, you'll agree that a beginners guide is irreplaceable. This is where this book comes in; to introduce you to 3D printing. You'll be guided throughout the whole process of designing and printing a 3D object.

You'll also learn how to troubleshoot your 3D printer as a beginner, tips and tricks for optimizing your 3D printer, and finally how to maintain your printer.

The last chapter of the book discusses briefly how to use SketchUp as a beginner.

Good enough, the author, a tech researcher and addict, explains the whole process of 3D printing in simple grammar syntax, as if he were writing for kids.

Now, enjoy the read!

CHAPTER 1

INTRODUCTION TO 3D PRINTING

I applaud you for taking the step to buy this book. I want to believe that you have already taken the step to buy/order a 3D printer. Kudos once more. You see, a 3D printer is a person not a thing. It actually is a combination of the person and the hardware that produces beautiful 3D models. Starting a 3D user journey can be tough but is equally rewarding. 3D printing spurs a beginner to exert himself as a maker, designer, scientist and artist. Tips and tricks may make the whole learning process easier but a beginner has to take each step himself. The most challenging part for anyone who's new to 3D printing is unboxing new hardware and executing the first successful print.

The 3D printing process basically changes a whole object into some thousands of tiny bit slices, and then slice by slice, it creates the object from the bottom. Those tiny pieces or layers gum together to form an object, a solid one. Coming home, imagine baking individual slices of bread and then gluing them together to form one big loaf (in lieu of the usual baking a big loaf and then slicing it). 3D printing is like baking individual bread slices and sticking them all together.

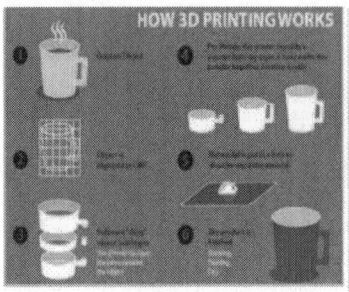

The most recent trend in 3D printing is having your face 3D printed and fit onto a Lego figure.

The 3D printing learning curve is steep. You need to be patient, yes very patient. You shouldn't get demotivated on the first print failures.

You need to also keep in mind that 3D printers come in various types. There are 3D printers that can print a single color at a time, there are those that can print a few colors at a time; and there are improved printers that offer full-spectrum prints.

Since you're just starting the 3D printing journey, all you need a 3D printer that prints a single color at a time. Now, let us delve into what 3D printing really is.

What really is 3D Printing?

This form of printing is also known as desktop fabrication or additive manufacturing. It involves creating a real, physical object based on a 3D design blueprint. 3D printing is clearly an emerging technology that was first introduced in 1986. Up till now, it has been attracting attention from all corners of the technology world. The very first machine capable of creating 3D objects from computer design was produced by 3D systems. The machine was named the Stereolithographic Apparatus. It used stereolithography as the process for printing 3D models. Following the creation of this machine, rapid developments have occurred in the area of 3D printing. Enough of history.

How a 3D printer works

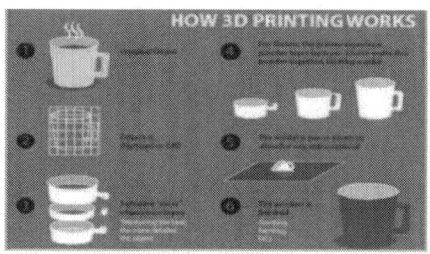

Normally, the 3D printer consists of a frame with the following axis:

X-axis (left to right movement)

Y-axis (front to back movement)

Z-axis (up and down movement)

An extruder is installed on the X-axis to feed the material that is used to create an object. The lowest part of the extruder is called the extruder head. This is where the filament is melted and extruded from a very small hole.

I believe you bought this book to learn about using a 3D printer. I will not delve into 3D printer hardware. In fact you do not necessary need to learn about all the parts and axis of a 3D printer to be able to use it.

Applications of 3D Printing

3D printing can be applied in the following fields;

Entertainment

Various kinds of prototypes of action figures, toys, musical equipment, games and other things are being created using 3D printers.

Automotive

This is yet another industry where 3D printing can be applied in. The automotive industry uses 3D printing technology for design verification and development of new engines.

Architecture

This industry uses 3D printing for design review, structure verification, expedited scaled modeling, and structure verification.

Manufacturing

3D printing has become a part of many manufacturing processes, including creating models of products before they are being manufactured in on a mass scale.

Defense

3D printing in the Defense sector is useful for making light-weight parts for surveillance equipment.

Education

3D printing technology provides a great method for geometry visualizations and design initiatives at art schools

Healthcare

3D printing has proved to be very valuable in the health industry. A number of working organs have been created and research is being carried out. We hope that sooner organs for transplant can be easily printed.

Home uses of a 3D printer

Fixing things around the house

With a 3D printer you can easily create parts for your appliances and devices if they break.

Making toys for your kids

There are a great number of model blueprints online. You can download them and print for your kids. The materials are basically similar to those used by creators of Lego. Your kids will love using 3D pens which are a good intro to 3D printing.

The following phone cases were printed from a 3D printer

Design for 3D Printing

3D printers let designers move from concept ideas and designs to physical models. The object will have to be designed on a computer using some sort of 3D design software. Immediately a part is designed, it can be imported into software specific to the 3D printer in use, which will slice the part and send the 3D printer a list of directions and paths used to create the part.

The numbers of CAD (Computer Aided Design) programs for designing 3D models for a variety of purposes are numerous. For a beginner, free software includes Autodesk 123D and Tinkercad. Once you progress in 3D design and printing, you might want to go for advanced software like SolidWorks and Autodesk Inventor.

CHAPTER 2

GETTING STARTED WITH 3D PRINTING

True, starting to use a 3D printer can be baffling. However, it isn't rocket science. This chapter focuses on providing insights that you'll need before plunging into the 3D printing world.

Do you need a 3D printer really?

Are you hoping to specialize in 3D printing or just wish to occasionally have some 3D printed objects around? Your answer to this question will determine what is best for you. If you don't hope to become a professional 3D designer, you might opt for online 3D design and printing services in lieu of doing it yourself. All you need do is send a blueprint of the object to any of these services. But if you really want to do it yourself, consider buying a 3D printer. Many 3D printers are sold for around $1000-$1500.

Once you buy a 3D printer, you have the choice of designing the blueprints of the object you want to 3D print, or getting them online ready-to-go. If you intend to get ready-to-go models, you can find them on the website called Thingiverse.

What if you decide to make your own models?

All you need is a Computer Aided Design (CAD) software. The latest in CAD software is even aimed at the ordinary user. However, because of the steep learning curve of the software, you'll need to spend a lot of time mastering the concept of 3D design and printing with CAD.

In order to learn the basics of 3D design, software like Autodesk 123D and Inventor Fusion are great options. Both software are free to use, but you would not have right to sell printed objects made from these free software. If you must do business with your 3D printing skills, ensure to invest in a commercial software license.

Is it possible to scan real objects and print them?

Yes, a big yes. You can scan and print objects. There are few companies that create dedicated 3D scanning equipment. An example is Go!SCAN 3D. Keep in mind, however, that the scanned models will need to be tweaked before being used to print objects. For, while the industry advances in technology, I advise you create your files with your own hand.

How can you print downloaded models?

Once you have downloaded model blueprints from websites like Thingiverse, you'll find out that they are still in STL format. For the printer to be able to handle the design files, they'll have to be sliced. This means it has to be transformed into the exact layer-by-layer description of the object, including the speed, wall thickness controls and temperature. The resulting file is called a G-Code, which can be interpreted by the printer.

There are a number of slicing applications out there. You'll have to pay for some of them, but the free ones include; ReplicatorG, Cura and KISSlicer.

How do you print models that you created?

You'll still need slicing software to create and print models. The slicing software program will be used to transform your model into a G-Code file.

On the other hand, if you used a 3D program like SketchUp, Photoshop or any other 3D design program that isn't designed for CAD, then the process of getting the G-Code file will require several steps.

First, you need to find out if the 3D model is genuinely printable or not. Most of the times, you'll need to make minor adjustments such as repairing vertices and patching up of holes.

Next, the file will need to be converted into an STL before it can be sliced for the printer. A free, open-source application that can help you patch up the model and generate the STL file is Meshlab. If you wish to opt for a commercial application, NetFabb is effective.

CHAPTER 3

HOW TO PRINT IN MULT-COLOR WITH A SINGLE EXTRUDER

Do you have a single extruder and wish to print in multi-color? Worry not! You heard that right? Worry not! There's a simple trick, using MatterControl, that'll help you print with rainbow colors. So how do you get started with multi-color printing? Consider the following easy steps:

Step 1

Open MatterControl and view the file to be printed. One the file is opened, you'll need to go to Layer View. Once you select Layer view, you'll be required to generate the layers for your file. All you need to do is to look at the lower part of the screen for the **Generate** option. Hit the **Generate** option and wait for your layers to load.

Step 2

The moment your layers have generated, MatterControl will show you print time. You'll need to divide your print time by the amount of colors you'll be using.

Let's assume it's a key chain you want to print, and you intend to use three colors. If the file is going to take 93 minutes to print, it means each color will print for 31 minutes approximately. I have a handy dandy timer on my phone. It's a great timer.

Step 3

Prepare your print space; have the three colors (or more) that you intend to use nearby. You should also know the order you want to print them in. the moment you have loaded your first color, hit print!

Step 4

You are going to need to start your timer. However, you shouldn't start your timer immediately you hit Print. Wait until your printer starts extruding, then you can start the timer.

Step 5

Once you are about one minute left you'll have to select **Settings & Controls** in MatterControl. When timer finally goes off, select the **Pause** button. When your print has paused, hit your Movement Controls and select Z+ between 2-3 times. You want to make sure you're not spending so much time in between pausing your print and moving your nozzle up. if you're too slow, your nozzle might melt your print in that one area.

Step 6

At this point, you'll need to change your filament. Simply release the extruder's cold end take out the current color. Load your new color. Make sure there are no clogs and push the filament through the hot end until you see the color change out the nozzle.

Step 7

The new color is now swapped in. select **Resume Print** button. Once you hit print you'll restart timer once more and wait for it to be up. Go through steps 4-8 for each color until all three colors have been used up.

Keep in mind that whether you're using the LulzBot Mini 3D printer or any single extrusion 3D printer all you need to create multi-color 3D printing is MatterControl. It can be downloaded for free at Matterhackers.com

To avoid melting your print when it is paused, simply add some code to automatically home the X/Y axis. Click **Settings** in **MatterControl**. Next, select **Printer** > **Custom G-Code,** and in the **Pause G-Code box** enter the following code: G28 X0 Y0; home X/Y axis (enter the quotes too).

Entering this code will automatically move the print head to the home position.

You can also enter the same command or code to the **Resume G-Code** box. That way, you're assured that your print will resume starting from the home position.

CHAPTER 4

3D PRINTING TIPS

The following tips will help you become acquainted with 3D printing

Get to know your printer

Sometimes, a printer can be delivered while not properly tuned. Try testing out all the different settings, printing different shapes with different settings. Taking these steps will help you become acquainted with your printer.

Ensure to check that everything is square, that the bed is level, that the belts are not loose. When you receive your printer, check for cracked glass build plates, bent rods or extruders that have been jostled out of alignment. Report any shipping related damages immediately.

Also, when you first get a 3D printer, try to print out lots of 20mm cubes. This will ensure you have a well calibrated machine.

Try to get everything vertically straight

The X, Y and Z axis of the printer should all be at angle 90 degree to each other. To accurately ensure this, after printing with a set square, printing cubes and testing them (measuring and checking if they are straight) is the best way to correctly check setup. Furthermore, you should ensure to always have your build plate calibrated. The filament must also always stick to the build plate – raft, tape, glue are great options to try.

Never try to print too many discrete objects at a time

It's not professional trying to print too many discrete objects at a time. Just one small widget that's being dragged around by your tool head can easily ruin an extensive multi-part print. Are you designing a model from the scratch? Ensure to test-print the tricky bits first by carving them out of the main model. Using Autodesk Meshmixer can help slice a complicated model up into bits.

Buy a little digital caliper

Digital calipers are sold for less than $10 on Amazon or Ebay. You will need them to calibrate your printer, accurately measure filament, and to adjust your utility.

Join a 3D printing forum

For you to really know what 3 printing is all about you'll need to join a great 3D printing forum. Usually, members of these groups share great tips and learning experiences. In the subsequent chapter, I'll list all the great 3D printing forums you can join.

Your ultimate aim should be to start designing using CAD

Some of the free/cheap programs that can help you to start modeling your own designs include; Autodesk Shapeshifter, Tinkercad, SketchUp etc. Trust me, you'll derive great satisfaction from modeling a design a 3D printing it yourself. You might decide to share or even sell them if they are wonderful.

Do not use transparent filament for your first print

Usually, clear filament is tough to photograph. You wouldn't want the very first photos you share of your models to be out of focus.

CHAPTER 5

COMMON 3D PRINTING TROUBLESHOOTING PROBLEMS AND SOLUTIONS

This chapter provides solution to common problems encountered in the 3D printing journey.

Troubleshooting for MatterControl Print Leveling

MatterControl introduced 7 and 13 point software print leveling around 2015. These options are fantastic for delta 3D printers and Cartesian printers with large print beds. For MatterControl's software leveling to function properly, there are some hardware and/or firmware settings needed. There are basically two configurations for 3D printers as it relates to endstops and leveling. They are Z Minimum and Z Maximum. I'll cover how to achieve proper leveling with MatterControl for both types.

Regardless of the type of print you're using, to get good leveling results, the nozzle of your hot end must be able to pinch a feeler gauge (or piece of paper) against the bed. If you're using a machine with a Z Minimum endstop setup – where the Z endstop triggers at the bed, Z=0- it is possible that one area of the bed may be below Z=0.

S ince many Z Minimum setups do not physically let movement past Z=0, it's unlikely that you'll get good leveling results without adjustments. If it's a Z Maximum setup you're using, it's likely there are firmware endstops that also prevent you from contacting the bed. However, both issues can be resolved easily.

Moany Delat printers use a Z Maximum endstop configuration. So the Z axis homes to the top of the build envelop, not to the bed. In order to prevent damage to the print bed, software endstops are often enabled in the firmware. These are set not to allow the machine go below Z=0.

By default, MatterControl does not allow you go below Z=0, but you can set Z to be negative.

Once you do that, configure the auto leveling through MatterControl. Once complete, click the pencil icon next to the **Automatic Print Leveling**.

A window will be opened displaying all of the sampled positions.

You should skim for negative Z value. If any of the positions have a negative, the firmware will prevent proper print leveling. So what do you do in case you see some negative Z values? It can be resolved. First, you'll need to find the lowest negative Z value. Let's say the negative z value is -1.52. You'll have to increase all the Z values by at least 1.52mm in order to get them out of negative range.

You can even increase by 2mm. use the Up/Down arrows on your keyboard to easily add/subtract 1mm. So, you'll need to click on every Z value – not just the negative values – and increase by 2mm.

Once you have done that, click Save in the bottom left corner of the window.

Next, you'll need to adjust Z height to account for the 2mm adjustment. Most firmware on Deltas have Z height in the EEPROM.

To access EEPROM, go to Options tab. Locate the Z height field. It's called Z Max Length on the machine.

At this point, you will need to increase by the same 2mm you increased the Auto Leveling numbers. In the bottom left corner, click save to EEPROM, and that's it; you're ready to print perfectly.

Z-Minimum Setup

Z-Min style machines don't commonly have issues with the auto leveling, but if yours does, you can resolve it by any of the fallowing ways:

1. Run Software Print Leveling by adjusting the height of your bed until it reaches the nozzle.

2. Adjust your Z endstop to allow the nozzle move lower. This, however, is recommended only on machines that home the Z axis with the nozzle positioned off to the side of the bed.

CHAPTER 6

TOOLS THAT WILL HELP YOU BECOME A 3D ORINTING PRO

As a beginner, the list below will make you become a pro within a short period of time.

3D SCANNER

You will almost need a 3D scanner if you want your 3D printing journey to be complete. 3D scanners generate 3D CAD models of real world objects. To scan objects, 3D scanners map points on the object to distances from the scanner. As a result, a 3D representation of the object is generated, which can be 3D printed.

KAPTON TAPE

This is a polyimide adhesive tape that is used as an alternative material to cover print beds. It has been specifically designed to withstand high temperatures (up to 400 degrees Celsius).

Kapton tape is used to improve 3D print adhesion and to prevent warping. It is also used to secure 3D printer components in the area of the hot end.

DIGITAL CALIPER

You will need this caliper for checking the precision of your prints as well as dimensioning parts that you wish to replicate in CAD software.

PALETTE KNIVES

I specifically have a need for palette knives when I'm faced with a 3D print that sticks to my print bed that cannot be removed by hand. In this case I simply use a palette knife to get under the print and pry it loose from the print bed.

GLUE STICK

You'll need glue ticks when you're trying to improve 3D print adhesion. All you need do is cover your print bed in water soluble glue stick. You can be rest assured that the 3D prints will improve immediately.

SAND PAPER

A great selection of sand paper, from coarse (220 grit) to fine (1000 grit), will be needed when post processing your 3D prints.

FLASHLIGHT

Except your 3D printer comes with integrated lighting, it is great to keep a flashlight nearby when 3D printing. The inside of enclosed 3D printers can be dark, even I well lit rooms. Using a compact LED light is perfect when checking prints.

LASER THERMOMETER

This is yet another tool that can come in handy under certain circumstances. If you're using a heated print bed, you may use it to cross check the heat setting of the slicer with the actual heat measured on the print bed surface. You'll also find the thermometer useful when trying to find out if the nozzle reaches the right temperature or whether outer edges of the heated print bed warm up evenly.

CHAPTER 7

3D PRINTING RESOURCES

This chapter covers a list of sites and free software that can make your 3D printing experience lit. Quickly, I'll start with the sites.

3D Model Sites

These sites are useful for sharing, buying and selling 3D printable designs. They include:

Pinshape.com

MyMiniFactory.com

Thingiverse.com

Shapeways.com

Free 3D Design Software

OpenSCAD

SketchUp

Tinkercad

Blender

Autodesk 123D

Slic3r

Skeinforge

CHAPTER 8

MAINTAINING YOUR 3D PRINTER

This is one section of the book you should take seriously. Your 3D printer needs to be properly cared for to function optimally. You'll need to give special attention to the plastic filament of your 3D printer. You cannot create anything without this filament. And once the quality of the filament begins to deteriorate, the quality of the end product might be compromised. So, how then can your 3D printer be kept in perfect working condition? Let us consider the things you need to do.

Tighten the Nuts and Bolts

Normally, the 3D printer mechanism is such that it can move. This movement can make the nuts and bolts to become loose with time. Loose nuts and bolts will only cause your 3D printer to wobble, thus affecting accuracy. Endeavor to tighten nuts and bolts every month. However, do not over tighten them.

Floss the Extruder Gear

You'll soon notice, with time, that some small pieces of plastic may accumulate in the extruder gear and prevent smooth rotation of the gear. Use a pointy object like needle or toothpick to remove such accumulation from the gear's teeth.

Oil the Rods

The three axis of the 3D printer (X, Y and Z) provide movement paths for the extruder head. For the end product to be accurate, movement must be smooth and unrestricted. Consequently, you should endeavor to oil the X, Y and Z rods every month.

This should be done after cleaning up any residue that you may find on them.

Check the Belt Tension

You should always test the belt tension and confirm it is correct. If there's a deviation, it will result in decrease in print quality. Adjust the belt tension as required (check the printer's manual for detailed direction on tightening belt tension).

Update Firmware

Firmware of 3D printers are improved regularly. Always check for any available updates for your extruder. Also, the software that you use in controlling the printer should also be updated (if any updates are available).

What you must never do with your 3D printer

Do not forget the hot nozzle

In order to melt the plastic filament, the nozzle of the extruder has to be hot. I mean very hot. It can exceed 150 degrees Celsius. If you must re-adjust the bed height during printing, keep in mind that the nozzle would be very hot. I'm sure you would not want even a little indentation in the printer bed.

Do not rush to using the 3D printer

When your 3D printer is delivered, you might become overly excited. That's not a problem, but do not start using it immediately. You might get something damaged. The best way is to start off slowly, go through the manual, taking one step at a time.

Check that your 3D printer is calibrated properly

It is true that 3D p[printers now come pre-calibrated. However, during transportation things can shift. So, once your printer has been delivered, ensure to check the following:

- Printer correctly configured in software
- Clearance of nozzle from print bed
- Print bed dimension accurately loaded in the software.

CHAPTER 9

BEGINNERS LESSONS TO FOR USING SKETCHUP

Download the software

Creating a 3D object with SketchUp isn't rocket science. I want to believe you have downloaded the software. If you haven't, however, kindly visit http://www.sketchup.com/download. This software is available both as free software and as paid one. The free software is ideal for beginners. But once you become a pro, you can opt for the paid version of SketchUp.

Prepare the workspace

SketchUp allows you to choose the workspace you want to use from a window that appears when you launch the app. You'll see three tabs on the window: **Learn**, **License**, and **Template**. The Template tab shows a list of various presets to select from.

The templates/presets differ in edge styles and backgrounds. Endeavor to explore all the templates for your training. I'll be starting with the very simple Template called **Meters**.

- Click on the **Meters** template, and then the button **Start using SketchUp** (you'll find this on the lower right side of the window).
- Next, I recommend that you check the box on the lower left side of the window that says **Always show on startup**. Checking the box will enable you to select any template each time you launch the application.

View the most important tools

SketchUp has lots of commands and tools that you can select from. You'll see default toolbars on the upper part of the screen on your first SketchUp workspace.

- Click on **View** > **Toolbars**. A window will appear, list toolbars. In this text, we used the **Large Tool Set**. This toolbar has almost every tool you'll need to finish a 3D model.
- Check the **Large Tool Set**, and uncheck the other toolbars to prevent confusion.

The Axes

Like any other 3D software, SketchUp makes use of Green, Blue and Red axes in the workspace. This makes it possible for you to view your work from different angles. You might also notice that SketchUp has a snapping feature, which helps align your lines or models along the different axes.

At this point, our toolbars are ready and our three-dimensional space with its three axes are before us. it's time to start creating our 2S shapes.

CHAPTER 10

HOW TO HANDLE BASIC 2D DRAWINGS – LINES, CIRCLES, RECTANGLES

Since we are just beginning the journey, let's start with drawing **Lines**, **Circles**, and **Rectangles**. These are fundamental to achieving success with 3D drawings.

Drawing Lines

To draw a line, do the following:

- Click the **Pencil** symbol on the toolbar or you can just tap **L** on your keyboard.
- Next, click anywhere on your screen to assign the first point. Then drag the mouse to any location of your choice (this will be the second point)

- You'll need to specify a length. To do this, enter a number (try entering 5). The number should be typed right after step 2, and then press **Enter**.

Drawing Circles

To draw a circle, do the following:

- Click the icon below the rectangle icon or just tap **C** on your keyboard.
- Click any desired point to assign the midpoint of your circle. Drag the cursor anywhere on the screen to make a Circle and then click.
- You'll need to specify the radius. To do this, enter the value (i.e 2) after step 2.

Drawing Rectangles/Squares

To draw a rectangle or square, do the following:

- Click thee Rectangle icon on the left, close to the pencil symbol. Alternatively, tap on R on your keyboard.
- Next, click the desired location to assign the first corner of your rectangle. Drag the cursor to the desired location for the opposite corner and click.
- You'll need to enter the length and width of your rectangle. Simply enter a value. Well, since you're creating a Rectangle, entering values might be a little tricky. Let's say you want to enter the number, 4. You'll enter the values this way: 4, 4. This is because the first value corresponds to the length/width along the Red axis and the second value corresponds to the length/width along the Green axis.

CONCLUSION

In this text, we have been able to discuss 3D printing process for beginners. In summary, we have seen that the steps involved in designing a 3D model are

The idea

As earlier pointed out, you need to decide what object you want to create. Is it a simple decoration or a complex toy? Anyways, I'll advice that you start with something simpler.

Designing the model

After deciding what object you want to make, the next major step is using CAD software or whatever software that can help you craft the model. In case you decided to use a CAD software, I always recommend Autodesk.

Converting it to STL

This will be a necessary thing to do if you're using non CAD software, such as Google SketchUp. You will need to convert design into STL format. Cadspan is a plugin you will need to install in order to be able to tweak and convert the final design.

Slicing it

You cannot avoid slicing up the model into layers. This is the only way the 3D printer can understand how to go about creating the object. This basically is the final step involving the use of computer software. It is at this stage that you will get the final G-Code file that the printer will recognize.

Printing

The 3D printer is ready to execute the task of 3D printing.

DISCLAIMER

In as much as the author believes beginners will find this book helpful in learning how to 3D print, it is only a small book. It should not be relied upon solely for all 3D printing tricks and troubleshooting. s

ABOUT THE AUTHOR

Stephen Rock has been a certified apps developer and tech researcher for more than 12 years. Some of his 'how to' guides have appeared in a handful of international journals and tech blogs. He loves rabbits.

Made in the USA
San Bernardino, CA
04 May 2020